MathStart®

NEGATIVE NUMBERS

# Less Than Zero

by Stuart J. Murphy

illustrations by Frank Remkiewicz

HarperCollinsPublishers

LEVEL
3

The publisher and author would like to thank teachers Patricia Chase, Phyllis Goldman, and Patrick Hopfensperger for
their help in making the math in MathStart just right for kids.

HarperCollins®, 🎒®, and MathStart® are registered trademarks of HarperCollins Publishers. For more information about the
MathStart series, write to HarperCollins Children's Books, 1350 Avenue of the Americas, New York, NY 10019,
or visit our website at www.mathstartbooks.com.

Bugs incorporated in the MathStart series design were painted by Jon Buller.

Less Than Zero

Library of Congress Cataloging-in-Publication Data
Murphy, Stuart J.
    Less than zero / by Stuart J. Murphy : illustrated by Frank Remkiewicz.
        p.        cm. — (MathStart)
    "Negative numbers, level 3."
    Summary: While trying to save enough money to buy a new ice scooter, Perry the penguin learns about managing his money and about
negative numbers.
ISBN 0-06-000124-0 — ISBN 0-06-000126-7 (pbk.)
    1. Arithmetic—Juvenile literature.    2. Numbers, Negative—Juvenile literature.    3. Arithmetic—Graphic methods—Juvenile literature.
[1. Arithmetic.    2. Numbers, Negative.    3. Finance, Personal.]    I. Remkiewicz, Frank, ill    II. Title.    III. Series.
QA107.2 .M87    2003                                                                                                                2002020732
513—dc21

Typography by Elynn Cohen    3 4 5 6 7 8 9 10    ❖    First Edition

To Heather,
who zeroes in and gets it done
—S.J.M.

For Pam Brown,
penguin lover and proud of it
—F.R.

All of Perry's friends had ice scooters. They could zip to school and zoom to the ice rink. Fuzzy could do figure eights. Baldy could even do flips.

Perry wanted a scooter too. But his dad said Perry would have to save 9 clams and buy one for himself.

"And I don't have a clam to my name," Perry moaned. "Not one clam!"

On Monday morning, Perry's mom said, "I'll pay you **4** clams to trim the ice in front of the house."

"That's hard work," said Perry.

"And that's a lot of clams," said Mom.

Perry trimmed all afternoon.

By the end of the day Perry had **4** clams of his own. He picked up a pad of paper and decided to make a graph to keep track of how many clams he had.

Perry wrote Sunday and Monday at the top. He made marks for **4** clams up the side. He made a big dot below Sunday at zero and another big dot below Monday on the line that showed **4** clams. Then he drew a line to connect the two dots.

*Wow! I've gone from zero to 4 clams in just one day!* he thought.

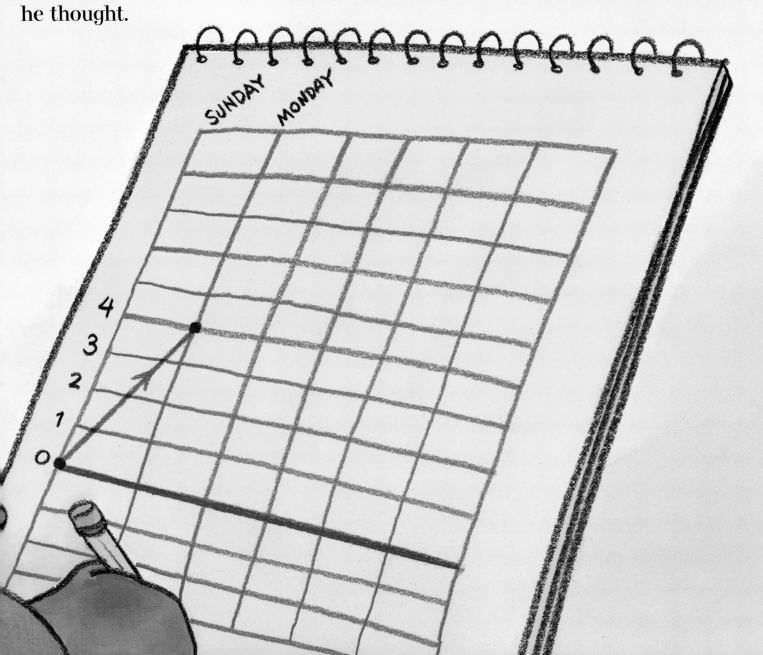

On Tuesday morning, Perry's friend Fuzzy called. "Do you want to go to the Ice Circus?" he asked. "It costs 5 clams."

The Ice Circus had seal acrobats and polar bear clowns and giant snow cones. Perry wanted to go more than anything. "But I only have 4 clams," he told Fuzzy.

"I can loan you 1 clam until next week," Fuzzy said.

The Ice Circus was fantastic!

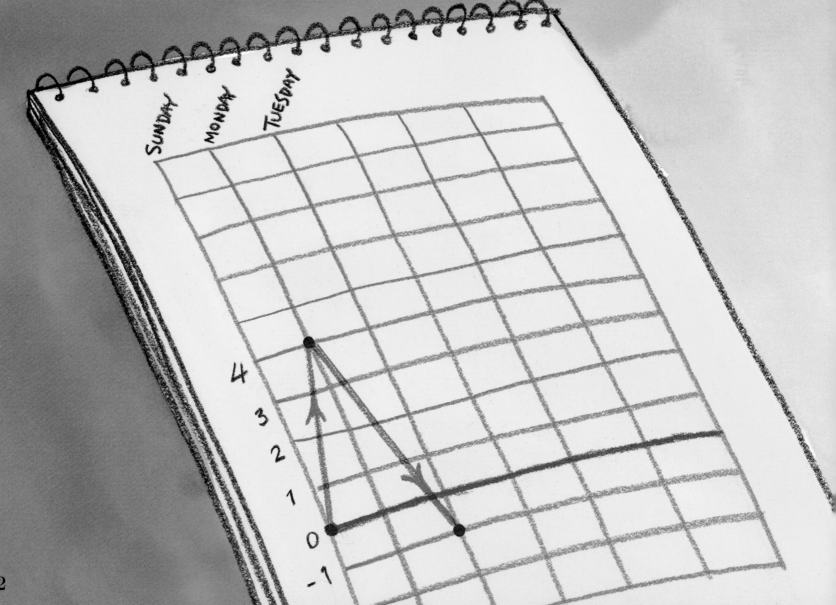

When Perry got home, he took out his pad of paper. He had spent his **4** clams, plus **1** more of Fuzzy's.

He wrote Tuesday at the top of the graph. Then he counted down **5** lines to show the clams he had spent. He wrote -1 below the zero. Then he made a big dot below Tuesday at the -1 line and drew a line from Monday's dot to Tuesday's.

*Gosh,* thought Perry. *I went from **4** clams to minus 1. That's even less than zero!*

At the end of ice-skating practice the next day, the Fishy Treat Truck was parked right by the gate. All of Perry's friends went zipping over on their scooters.

"C'mon," said Baldy. "Let's get a treat."

"But I don't have any clams," said Perry. "And I already owe Fuzzy 1 clam."

"Well, I can loan you 2 clams for a Fishy Float," Baldy said.

Perry couldn't resist. "Sardine's my favorite," he said.

It was delicious.

That night Perry took out his pad of paper again.

Perry counted down 2 more lines to show the clams he had borrowed from Baldy. Below -1 he wrote -2 and -3.

Then he wrote Wednesday at the top, made a big dot on the -3 line, and drew a line from Tuesday's dot to Wednesday's.

*Oh no*, thought Perry. *Now I'm 3 clams less than zero!*

The next morning Perry didn't go outside. All his friends were playing on their ice scooters. It was no fun just watching.

Perry lay down on the floor and sighed. Then something under the couch caught his eye.

It was a clam!

*Wow!* he thought. *Maybe there are more clams hidden around the house.*

Perry started a clam search. He looked everywhere—behind the rewarmerator, over the cooling oven, even in the big ice chest. By the end of the day he had found 8 clams. And his dad said he could keep them.

Perry ran to his room and took out his pad.

Perry wrote Thursday at the top. Then he counted up 8 lines to show the clams he had found and made a dot below Thursday at the line that meant 5 clams.

He drew a line from Wednesday's dot to Thursday's.

When I pay back the 3 clams I owe Baldy and Fuzzy, I'll only have *5 clams left*, thought Perry. *I wish I hadn't borrowed those clams!*

The next afternoon Perry put all his clams in his pocket and went out to meet Baldy and Fuzzy. But when he reached into his pocket, there was nothing in it! He felt and felt, but all he could feel was a great big hole.

"Oh no," moaned Perry. "I can't believe it. I lost 8 whole clams."
Fuzzy and Baldy helped him look until it started to get dark.
But there wasn't a clam in sight.

When he got home, Perry went into his room. He took out his pad sadly.

Perry wrote Friday on the top. He counted down 8 lines and made a big dot below Friday on the -3 line.

Then he connected Thursday's dot to Friday's.

*I'm right back where I was on Wednesday*, thought Perry.

"So long, scooter," he whispered as he drifted off to sleep.

In the morning, Mr. Spike from next door was in the kitchen when Perry woke up.

"Hello there, Perry," said Mr. Spike. "Remember when you waved to me yesterday while I was shoveling snow?"

"Uh-huh," Perry answered sleepily.

"Look what I found after you left." Mr. Spike reached into his pocket and handed 8 clams to Perry.

Perry ran to get his pad.

27

Perry counted up 8 lines and made a big dot on the line that showed 5 clams.

Then he connected Friday's dot to Saturday's.

After he paid back Fuzzy and Baldy, he would have 5 clams left.

"Not only that," added Mr. Spike, "your parents told me that you want to buy an ice scooter, and I need some help shoveling snow. How many clams do you need? I'll give them to you now, and you can work them off later."

The scooter cost 9 clams.

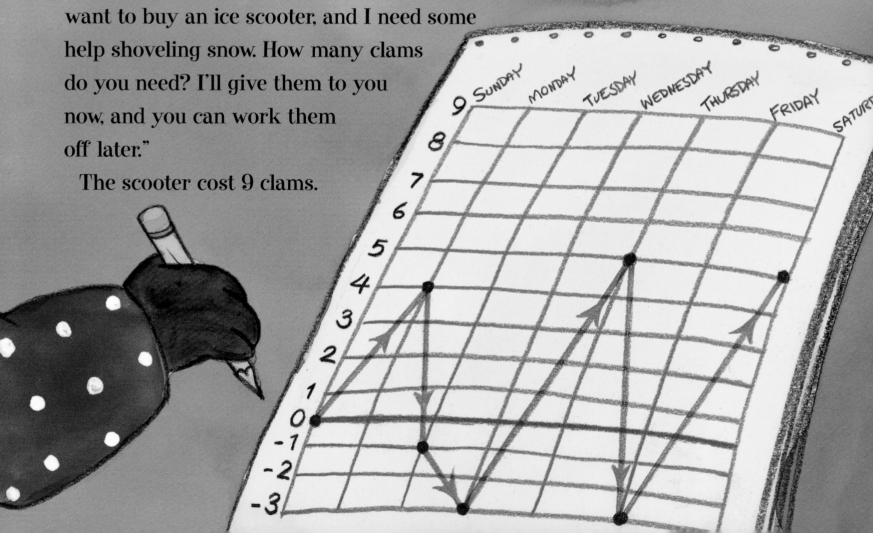

Perry counted up 4 lines and made another big dot on the 9
line. He connected the dots.

"I need 4 more clams to buy the scooter," Perry told Mr. Spike.
Mr. Spike handed Perry 4 clams. "If you shovel snow for me for 4
days, we'll be even," he said.

29

It was Sunday again, and the Fishy Treats Truck was open for business.

"Get your Fishy Fries here," yelled the seal. "Only 3 clams."

"Want some?" asked Fuzzy.

"I can loan you some clams," offered Baldy.

"No way," said Perry. "I already have 4 clams less than zero. That's what I owe Mr. Spike. But I do have a cool new scooter— and a cool new job, too."

And Perry scooted off to shovel snow.

In *Less Than Zero*, the math concept is negative numbers. The introduction of negative numbers extends a child's knowledge of our number system and aids in the development of algebraic concepts.

If you would like to have more fun with the math concepts presented in *Less Than Zero*, here are a few suggestions:

- After reading the story, return to the graphs. Have the child retell the story by looking at the graphs to see what happened to Perry's clams.

- Have the child pretend that he or she is Perry and is saving for an ice scooter. Act out the story, using buttons or other small objects to represent the clams. Change the number of objects to mirror the number of clams involved in the transactions, and have the child make a graph similar to the one shown in the story.

- Create a number line like the one shown below. As you reread the story, keep track of Perry's clams by using a marker (a button or a penny will also work) on the number line. Start with the marker on zero. When Perry gains some clams, move the marker to the right to reach the correct number. When Perry spends or loses his clams, move the marker to the left to change the number. After each move, ask, "How many clams does Perry have now?"

-4  -3  -2  -1  0  1  2  3  4  5  6  7  8  9  10

Following are some activities that will help you extend the concepts presented in *Less Than Zero* into a child's everyday life:

**Tracking Money:** Have the child write down the amount of his or her allowance in a notebook. Then have him or her keep a running account of the funds as they are spent. Discuss what could happen if he or she wants to make a purchase after the allowance is spent.

**Mapping the Neighborhood:** Draw a map that shows the distance from your house to a park or a local place of interest. Label the distance in blocks or other even segments. Using a marker or a finger, have the child "walk" 2 blocks forward on the map. Ask, "How many blocks are we from the park?" Then have the child "walk" 1 block back and ask, "Now how far are we from the park?" Then try the activity this way: Think of the starting place (your house) as zero, and help the child figure out how to use negative and positive numbers to describe how far he or she is from the park or from home.

The following books include some of the same concepts that are presented in *Less Than Zero*:

- MR. MONOPOLY'S AMUSEMENT PARK by Jackie Glassman
- A PLACE FOR ZERO: A MATH ADVENTURE by Angeline Sparagna Lopresti
- ZERO: IS IT SOMETHING? IS IT NOTHING? by Claudia Zaslavsky